Favourite
BRITISH
Recipes

**FLAME TREE
PUBLISHING**

Contents

Introduction

'The dinner is the happy end of the Briton's day. We work harder than the other nations of the earth. We do more, we live more in our time... Every great man amongst us likes his dinner, and takes to it kindly.'

Extract from *The Book of Snobs*
by William Makepeace Thackeray (1811–63)

Nothing beats a good Sunday roast with succulent beef, airy Yorkshire puds and all the trimmings, or walking along the seaside with delicious fish and chips enhanced with a splash of salt and vinegar. Food can transport you anywhere – a comforting jam roly poly and custard might take you back to your grandmother's teas, or a classic drink of Pimm's will remind you of sitting in the park watching the cricket. These recipes have made their way into the British national identity, conjuring up images of home and happiness.

In the seventeenth century, pies, puddings and roast beef all became the nation's favourite dishes. Hannah Woolley made her living from books on the subject of cookery and household management, starting a tradition which Mrs Beeton would famously follow in the nineteenth century, all the way up to the present day in which we still love to celebrate British cooking.

We've moved from roasting beef over spits in the fire to the modern day roast, but the love of the same enticing flavours hasn't changed. Just as our national dishes have evolved, so has the practice of British etiquette, so that table manners have become an important component of our mealtimes. Dining well is an important part of who we are.

This fun and practical book celebrates the best of British with those comforting and traditional meals that we all remember from our childhood and still love to indulge in. Along with this ultimate collection of recipes come hints, tips, facts and poems to delight.

Smoked Haddock Kedgeree

SERVES 4

1. Place the haddock in a shallow frying pan and cover with 300 ml/½ pint water. Simmer gently for 8–10 minutes until the fish is cooked. Drain, then remove all the skin and bones from the fish and flake into a dish. Keep warm.

2. Melt the butter in a saucepan and add the chopped onion and curry powder. Cook, stirring, for 3–4 minutes until the onion is soft, then stir in the rice. Cook for a further minute, stirring continuously, then stir in the hot stock.

3. Cover and simmer gently for 15 minutes, or until the rice has absorbed all the liquid. Cut the eggs into quarters or eighths and add half to the mixture with half the parsley.

4. Carefully fold in the cooked fish to the mixture and add the cream, if using. Season to taste with salt and pepper. Heat the kedgeree through briefly until piping hot.

5. Transfer the mixture to a large dish and garnish with the remaining eggs and parsley, and serve with a pinch of cayenne pepper. Serve immediately.

Ingredients

450 g/1 lb smoked haddock fillets
50 g/2 oz butter
1 onion, peeled and finely chopped
2 tsp mild curry powder
175 g/6 oz long-grain rice
450 ml/ ³/₄ pint fish or vegetable stock, heated
2 large eggs, hard-boiled and shelled
2 tbsp freshly chopped parsley
2 tbsp whipping cream (optional)
salt and freshly ground black pepper
pinch cayenne pepper

Cullen Skink

SERVES 6-8

1. Melt the butter in a large, heavy-based saucepan, add the onion and sauté for 3 minutes, stirring occasionally. Add the bay leaf and stir, then sprinkle in the flour and cook over a low heat for 2 minutes, stirring frequently. Add the potatoes.

2. Take off the heat and gradually stir in the milk and 300 ml/1/2 pint water. Return to the heat and bring to the boil, stirring. Reduce the heat to a simmer and cook for 10 minutes.

3. Meanwhile, discard any pin bones from the fish and cut into small pieces. Add to the pan together with the sweetcorn and peas. Cover and cook gently, stirring occasionally, for 10 minutes, or until the vegetables and fish are cooked.

4. Add pepper and nutmeg to taste, then stir in the cream and heat gently for 1–2 minutes until piping hot. Sprinkle with the parsley and serve with crusty bread.

Ingredients

25 g/1 oz unsalted butter
1 onion, peeled and chopped
1 fresh bay leaf
25 g/1 oz plain flour
350 g/12 oz new potatoes, scrubbed and cut
    into small pieces
600 ml/1 pint semi-skimmed milk
350 g/12 oz undyed smoked haddock fillet, skinned
75 g/3 oz sweetcorn kernels
50 g/2 oz garden peas
freshly ground black pepper
1/2 tsp freshly grated nutmeg
2–3 tbsp single cream
2 tbsp freshly chopped parsley
crusty bread, to serve

Napkin Folding

Make an elegant fan shape out of your napkin that will stand on the table.

1. It may help to iron your napkin first. Take the napkin and spread it out in front of you. Fold it in half and turn the napkin so that the open end is furthest from you.

2. Starting from the right, fold the napkin like a concertina. Stop about a third before the end, with the folds on the top, as this last bit will form the stand of the fan.

3. Fold the napkin in half vertically, folding the bottom half under the top, keeping the concertina folds on the outside.

4. You should have ended up with two free corners of the material. Fold these diagonally towards you, so that you can tuck them under the concertina folds.

5. Let go to open up your fan and let it stand on the table.

Cawl

SERVES 6-8

1. Put the lamb in a large saucepan, cover with cold water and bring to the boil. Add a generous pinch of salt. Simmer gently for 1½ hours, then set aside to cool completely, preferably overnight.

2. The next day, skim the fat off the surface of the lamb liquid and discard. Return the saucepan to the heat and bring back to the boil. Simmer for 5 minutes. Add the onions, potatoes, parsnips, swede and carrots and return to the boil. Reduce the heat, cover and cook for about 20 minutes, stirring occasionally.

3. Add the leeks and season to taste with salt and pepper. Cook for a further 10 minutes, or until all the vegetables are tender.

4. Using a slotted spoon, remove the meat from the saucepan and take the meat off the bone. Discard the bones and any gristle, then return the meat to the pan. Adjust the seasoning to taste, stir in the parsley, then serve immediately with plenty of warm crusty bread.

Ingredients

700 g/1½ lb scrag end of lamb or best end
   of neck chops
pinch salt
2 large onions, peeled and thinly sliced
3 large potatoes, peeled and cut into chunks
2 parsnips, peeled and cut into chunks
1 swede, peeled and cut into chunks
3 large carrots, peeled and cut into chunks
2 leeks, trimmed and sliced
salt and freshly ground black pepper
4 tbsp freshly chopped parsley
warm crusty bread, to serve

Battered Cod & Chunky Chips

SERVES 4

1. Dissolve the yeast with a little of the beer in a jug and mix to a paste. Pour in the remaining beer, whisking all the time until smooth. Place the flour and salt in a bowl, and gradually pour in the beer mixture, whisking continuously to make a thick smooth batter. Cover the bowl and allow the batter to stand at room temperature for 1 hour.

2. Peel the potatoes and cut into thick slices. Cut each slice lengthways to make chunky chips. Place them in a nonstick frying pan and heat, shaking the pan until all the moisture has evaporated. Turn them onto absorbent kitchen paper to dry off.

3. Heat the oil in the pan to 180°C/350°F, then fry the chips a few at a time for 4–5 minutes until crisp and golden. Drain on absorbent kitchen paper and keep warm.

4. Pat the cod fillets dry, then coat in the seasoned flour. Dip the fillets into the reserved batter. Fry for 2–3 minutes until cooked and crisp, then drain. Garnish with lemon wedges and parsley and serve immediately with the chips, tomato ketchup and vinegar.

Ingredients

15 g/½ oz fresh yeast
300 ml/½ pint beer
225 g/8 oz plain flour
1 tsp salt
700 g/1½ lb potatoes
450 ml/¾ pint groundnut oil
4 cod fillets, about 225 g/8 oz each, skinned and boned
2 tbsp seasoned plain flour

To garnish:
lemon wedges
flat-leaf parsley sprigs

To serve:
tomato ketchup
vinegar

Leek & Potato Tart

SERVES 6

1. Preheat the oven to 200°C/400°F/Gas Mark 6, about 15 minutes before baking. Sift the flour and salt into a bowl. Rub in the butter until the mixture resembles breadcrumbs. Stir in the nuts. Mix together the egg yolk and 3 tablespoons cold water. Sprinkle over the dry ingredients. Mix to form a dough.

2. Knead on a lightly floured surface for a few seconds, then wrap in clingfilm and chill in the refrigerator for 20 minutes. Roll out and use to line a 20.5 cm/8 inch springform tin or very deep flan tin. Chill for a further 30 minutes.

3. Cook the leeks in the butter over a high heat for 2–3 minutes, stirring constantly. Lower the heat, cover and cook for 25 minutes until soft, stirring occasionally. Remove the leeks from the heat.

4. Cook the potatoes in boiling salted water for 15 minutes, or until almost tender. Drain and thickly slice. Add to the leeks. Stir the sour cream into the leeks and potatoes, followed by the eggs, cheese, nutmeg and salt and pepper. Pour into the pastry case and bake on the middle shelf in the preheated oven for 20 minutes.

5. Reduce the oven temperature to 190°C/375°F/Gas Mark 5 and cook for a further 30–35 minutes until the filling is set.
Garnish with chives and serve immediately.

Ingredients

225 g/8 oz plain flour
pinch salt
150 g/5 oz butter, cubed
50 g/2 oz walnuts, very finely chopped
1 large egg yolk

For the filling:
450 g/1 lb leeks, trimmed and thinly sliced
40 g/1½ oz butter
450 g/1 lb large new potatoes, scrubbed
300 ml/½ pint sour cream
3 medium eggs, lightly beaten
175 g/6 oz Gruyère cheese, grated
freshly grated nutmeg
salt and freshly ground black pepper
fresh chives, to garnish

Cornish Pasties

SERVES 4

1. Preheat the oven to 180°C/350°F/Gas Mark 4, about 15 minutes before required. For the pastry, sift the flour into a large bowl and add the fats, chopped into little pieces. Rub the fats and flour together until the mixture resembles coarse breadcrumbs. Season to taste with salt and pepper and mix again.

2. Add about 2 tablespoons cold water, a little at a time, and mix until the mixture comes together to form a firm but pliable dough. Turn onto a lightly floured surface, knead until smooth, then wrap and chill in the refrigerator.

3. For the filling, put the steak in a large bowl with the onion. Add the potatoes and swede to the bowl together with the Worcestershire sauce and more salt and pepper. Mix well.

4. Divide the dough into eight balls and roll each ball into a circle about 25.5 cm/10 inches across. Divide the filling between the circles of pastry. Wet the edge of the pastry, then fold over the filling. Pinch the edges to seal.

5. Transfer the pasties to a lightly oiled baking sheet. Make a couple of small holes in each pasty and brush with beaten egg. Cook in the oven for 15 minutes, remove and brush again with the egg. Return to the oven for a further 15–20 minutes until golden. Cool slightly, garnish with tomato and parsley and serve.

Ingredients

For the pastry:
350 g/12 oz self-raising flour
75 g/3 oz butter or margarine
75 g/3 oz lard or white vegetable fat
salt and freshly ground black pepper

For the filling:
550 g/1¼ lb braising steak, chopped very finely
1 large onion, peeled and finely chopped
1 large potato, peeled and diced
200 g/7 oz swede, peeled and diced
3 tbsp Worcestershire sauce
1 small egg, beaten, to glaze

To garnish:
tomato slices or wedges
fresh parsley sprigs

Salmon Fish Cakes

SERVES 4

1. Cube the potatoes and cook in lightly salted boiling water for 15 minutes. Drain and mash the potatoes. Place in a mixing bowl and reserve.

2. Place the salmon in a food processor and blend to form a chunky purée. Add the purée to the potatoes and mix together.

3. Coarsely grate the carrot and add to the fish with the lemon zest and coriander.

4. Add the egg yolk, season to taste with salt and pepper, then gently mix the ingredients together. With damp hands, form the mixture into four large fish cakes.

5. Coat in the flour and place on a plate. Cover loosely and chill for at least 30 minutes.

6. When ready to cook, spray a griddle pan with a few fine sprays of oil and heat the pan. When hot add the fish cakes and cook on both sides for 3–4 minutes until the fish is cooked. Add an extra spray of oil if needed during the cooking.

7. When the fish cakes are cooked, serve immediately with the tomato sauce, green salad and crusty bread.

Ingredients

225 g/8 oz potatoes, peeled
450 g/1 lb salmon fillet, skinned
125 g/4 oz carrot, trimmed and peeled
2 tbsp grated lemon zest
2–3 tbsp freshly chopped coriander
1 medium egg yolk
salt and freshly ground black pepper
2 tbsp plain white flour
few fine sprays oil

To serve:
prepared tomato sauce
tossed green salad
crusty bread

Lancashire Hotpot

SERVES 4

1. Preheat the oven to 170°C/325°F/Gas Mark 3. Trim any excess fat from the lamb cutlets. Heat the oil in a frying pan and brown the cutlets in batches for 3–4 minutes. Remove with a slotted spoon and reserve.

2. Add the onions to the frying pan and cook for 6–8 minutes until softened and just beginning to colour. Stir in the flour and cook for a few seconds, then gradually pour in the stock, stirring well, and bring to the boil. Remove from the heat.

3. Spread the base of a large casserole dish with half the potato slices. Top with half the onions and season well with salt and pepper. Arrange the browned meat in a layer. Season again and add the remaining onions, bay leaf and thyme. Pour in the remaining liquid from the onions and top with remaining potatoes so that they overlap in a single layer. Brush the potatoes with the melted butter and season again.

4. Cover the saucepan and cook in the preheated oven for 2 hours, uncovering for the last 30 minutes to allow the potatoes to brown. Garnish with chopped herbs and serve immediately with green beans.

Ingredients

1 kg/2¼ lb middle end neck of lamb,
   divided into cutlets
2 tbsp vegetable oil
2 large onions, peeled and sliced
2 tsp plain flour
150 ml/¼ pint vegetable or lamb stock
700 g/1½ lb waxy potatoes,
   peeled and thickly sliced
salt and freshly ground black pepper
1 bay leaf
2 fresh thyme sprigs
1 tbsp melted butter
2 tbsp freshly chopped herbs, to garnish
freshly cooked green beans, to serve

Food Named After Brits

Earl Grey Tea
The popular tea flavoured with bergamot is named after Charles, 2nd Earl Grey, Prime Minister of 1830–34. A popular tale is that Grey was sent a gift of this particular blend by a grateful Chinese man, whose life had been saved by a diplomatic envoy Grey had sent.

Bloody Mary
There are a number of Marys linked to the naming of this cocktail, however one possible origin is Queen Mary I of England, nicknamed Bloody Mary for her Catholic zeal in burning heretics.

Beef Wellington
It is generally thought that this dish of beef coated in pâté and baked in pastry is named after the Duke of Wellington Arthur Wellesley, best known for defeating Napoleon at the Battle of Waterloo.

Victoria Sponge
It was during the time of Queen Victoria that the tradition of teatime became popular in England. The sponge cake was named after Queen Victoria in her honour.

Sandwich
John Montagu, the Earl of Sandwich, ordered a servant to fetch him some beef placed between slices of bread so that he didn't have to stop playing cards in order to eat. Thereafter it became popular to ask for 'a sandwich'.

Top Tip

Can't remember which of the side plates is yours?
Here is a handy way to remember the rule:
Discretely make the thumbs up signs with your hands. The left
hand resembles a 'b' for bread, to show that your bread dish is the
side dish to your left. Also, the right hand resembles a 'd' to
indicate your drinks glasses are set to your right.

Shepherd's Pie

SERVES 4

1. Preheat the oven to 200°C/400°F/Gas Mark 6, about 15 minutes before cooking. Heat the oil in a large saucepan and add the onion, carrot and celery. Cook over a medium heat for 8–10 minutes until softened and starting to brown.

2. Add the thyme and cook briefly, then add the cooked lamb, wine, stock and tomato purée. Season to taste with salt and pepper and simmer gently for 25–30 minutes until reduced and thickened. Remove from the heat to cool slightly and season again.

3. Meanwhile, boil the potatoes in plenty of salted water for 12–15 minutes until tender. Drain and return to the saucepan over a low heat to dry out. Remove from the heat and add the butter, milk and parsley. Mash until creamy, adding a little more milk, if necessary. Adjust the seasoning.

4. Transfer the lamb mixture to a shallow ovenproof dish. Spoon the mash over the filling and spread evenly to cover completely. Fork the surface, place on a baking sheet, then cook in the preheated oven for 25–30 minutes until the potato topping is browned and the filling is piping hot. Garnish and serve.

Ingredients

2 tbsp vegetable or olive oil
1 onion, peeled and finely chopped
1 carrot, peeled and finely chopped
1 celery stalk, trimmed and finely chopped
1 tbsp fresh thyme leaves
450 g/1 lb leftover roast lamb, finely chopped
150 ml/¼ pint red wine
150 ml/¼ pint lamb or vegetable
    stock or leftover gravy
2 tbsp tomato purée
salt and freshly ground black pepper
700 g/1½ lb potatoes, peeled and
    cut into chunks
25 g/1 oz butter
6 tbsp milk
1 tbsp freshly chopped
    parsley
fresh herbs, to garnish

Roast Beef & Yorkshire Puds

SERVES 6-8

1. Preheat the oven to 220°C/425°F/Gas Mark 7, 15 minutes before required. Trim the joint, discarding any excess fat. (There needs to be a little fat on the joint to ensure the meat is moist.) Tie firmly with string to ensure the joint keeps its shape during roasting. If the meat is on the bone, allow 20 minutes per 450 g/1 lb plus 20 minutes, for rare; 25 minutes plus 25 minutes for medium; and 30 minutes plus 30 minutes for well done. (If the meat is boned and rolled, allow 25 minutes per 450 g/1 lb plus 25 for rare; 30 minutes plus 30 for medium; and 35 minutes plus 35 for well done.) Season the joint and place in a roasting tin. Roast for the calculated time.

2. While the beef is cooking, make the Yorkshire pudding batter. Sift the flour and salt into a bowl. Make a well in the centre and add the eggs and a little of the milk. Beat to form a smooth batter, drawing in the flour and gradually stirring in the milk. Allow to stand for at least 30 minutes.

3. When the beef is cooked, remove from the oven (keeping the oven on) and place on a serving platter, keeping the meat juices in the tin. Cover with foil and a clean towel to rest for 10–15 minutes before carving. To cook the Yorkshires, pour a little oil into 6–8 holes of a bun tray and place in the oven. Heat for 3–5 minutes until the oil is almost smoking. Stir the batter and, when the oil is hot enough, pour into the tray. Place in the oven and cook for 15 minutes, or until well risen and puffy. Meanwhile, make the gravy by placing the tin of juices on the hob. Heat for 1–2 minutes until bubbling. Sprinkle in the flour, if using, and cook for 2 minutes, stirring constantly. Carefully pour in the stock and continue stirring until it has thickened slightly. Simmer, stirring occasionally, for 2 minutes, then pour into a jug. Serve the beef with the gravy, Yorkshire puddings, horseradish sauce, roasted potatoes and freshly cooked vegetables.

Ingredients

1 joint of beef, such as rib or top side, about 1.5 kg/3 lb 5 oz
salt and freshly ground black pepper

For the Yorkshire puddings:
125 g/4 oz plain flour; pinch salt; 2 medium eggs; 225 ml/8 fl oz milk;
1 tbsp sunflower oil

For the gravy:
1 tbsp plain flour (optional); 300 ml/¹⁄₂ pint beef stock

To serve:
gravy, Yorkshire puddings, horseradish sauce, roasted potatoes, freshly cooked vegetables

Extract from 'The Roast Beef of Old England'

When mighty Roast Beef was the Englishman's food,
It ennobled our brains and enriched our blood.
Our soldiers were brave and our courtiers were good
Oh! the Roast Beef of old England,
And old English Roast Beef!

by Henry Fielding (1707–54)

Steak & Kidney Pie

SERVES 4-6

1. Preheat the oven to 160°C/325°F/Gas Mark 3, 10 minutes before required. Slice the halved kidneys. Heat the oil in a large saucepan over medium heat and add the onion. Cook, stirring, for 5 minutes and transfer to a plate. Add the steak and kidneys to the oil remaining in the pan and cook for 5–8 minutes until sealed.

2. Return the onion to the pan together with the carrots and sliced mushrooms. Sprinkle in the flour and cook for 2 minutes. Blend the tomato purée with a little of the stock and add to the pan. Stir in the remaining stock and the bay leaves. Bring to a boil. Transfer to a casserole dish and cook in the oven for 2 hours, or until tender.

3. Remove from the oven, discard the bay leaves, and season with black pepper. Using a slotted spoon, transfer the mixture into an ovenproof 1.1 litre/2 pint pie dish. Reserve the remaining liquid to use for gravy.

Ingredients

4–6 lambs' kidneys, halved and cores discarded
2 tbsp olive oil
1 medium onion, peeled and chopped
575 g/1¼ lb braising steak, trimmed and chopped
225 g/8 oz chopped carrots
75 g/3 oz sliced button mushrooms
25 g/1 oz plain flour
1 tbsp tomato purée
900 ml/1½ pints beef stock
2 fresh bay leaves
freshly ground black pepper
375 g/13 oz prepared puff pastry
1 small egg, beaten
roasted potatoes and Brussels sprouts, to serve

4. Roll the pastry out on a lightly floured surface and cut a 2.5 cm/1 inch wide strip long enough to go around the edge of the pie dish. Press firmly onto the rim of the dish. Roll the remaining pastry out to form a lid large enough to cover the pie dish. Lightly brush the pastry strip with a little beaten egg and place the lid on top. Press the two edges firmly together. Trim with a sharp knife. Use any remaining pastry to decorate the top of the pie. Brush lightly with some of the beaten egg and place on a baking tray. Let rest in the refrigerator for 30 minutes.

5. Preheat the oven to 220°C/425°F/Gas Mark 7. Cook the pie in the oven for 30–35 minutes until golden brown. Brush the crust again with the egg halfway through the cooking time. Reheat the remaining gravy and serve with the pie, along with the potatoes and Brussels sprouts.

Toad in the Hole

SERVES 4

1. Preheat the oven to 220°C/425°F/Gas Mark 7, 15 minutes before required. Lightly prick the sausages and reserve.

2. Sift the flour and salt into a mixing bowl and make a well in the centre. Drop the eggs into the well and then, using a wooden spoon, beat in the eggs, drawing the flour in from the sides of the bowl. Gradually add the milk and beat to form a smooth batter without any lumps. Let stand for 30 minutes.

3. When ready to cook, pour the oil into a 25.5 x 20.5 cm/10 x 8 inch roasting tin. Heat in the oven until almost smoking and then add the sausages. Carefully turn the sausages in the hot oil and return to the oven for 5 minutes.

4. Remove from the oven and turn them over again. Stir the batter well and pour over the sausages. Return to the oven and cook for 35–40 minutes until the pudding is well risen and golden brown. Serve immediately with seasonal vegetables and English mustard.

Ingredients

8 large pork sausages
125 g/4 oz plain flour
pinch salt
2 medium eggs
225 ml/8 fl oz milk
1 tbsp sunflower oil
seasonal vegetables and English
    mustard, to serve

Did You Know?

The first Sunday of every February is British Yorkshire Pudding Day.

Crown Roast of Lamb

SERVES 6

1. Preheat the oven to 180°C/350°F/Gas Mark 4, about 10 minutes before roasting. Wipe the crown roast and season the cavity with salt and pepper. Place in a roasting tin and cover the ends of the bones with small pieces of kitchen foil.

2. Heat the oil in a small saucepan and cook the onion, garlic and celery for 5 minutes, then remove the saucepan from the heat. Add the cooked rice with the apricots, pine nuts, orange zest and coriander. Season with salt and pepper, then stir in the egg and mix well.

3. Carefully spoon the prepared stuffing into the cavity of the lamb, then roast in the preheated oven for 1–1½ hours. Remove the lamb from the oven and remove and discard the foil from the bones. Return to the oven and continue to cook for a further 15 minutes, or until cooked to personal preference.

4. Remove from the oven and leave to rest for 10 minutes before serving with the roasted potatoes and freshly cooked green vegetables.

Ingredients

1 lamb crown roast
salt and freshly ground black pepper
1 tbsp sunflower oil
1 small onion, peeled and finely chopped
2–3 garlic cloves, peeled and crushed
2 celery stalks, trimmed and finely chopped
125 g/4 oz cooked mixed basmati and wild rice
75 g/3 oz ready-to-eat dried apricots, chopped
50 g/2 oz pine nuts, toasted
1 tbsp finely grated orange zest
2 tbsp freshly chopped coriander
1 small egg, beaten
freshly roasted potatoes and freshly cooked
    green vegetables, to serve

Chicken & Ham Pie

SERVES 6

1. Preheat the oven to 200°C/400°F/Gas Mark 6. Heat the oil in a frying pan and fry the leek and bacon for 4 minutes until soft but not coloured. Transfer to a bowl and reserve.

2. Cut the chicken into bite-size pieces and add to the leek and bacon. Toss the avocado in the lemon juice, add to the chicken and season to taste with salt and pepper.

3. Roll out half the pastry on a lightly floured surface and use to line an 18 cm/7 inch loose-bottomed deep flan tin. Scoop the chicken mixture into the pastry case.

4. Beat 1 egg and mix with the yogurt and the chicken stock. Pour the yogurt mixture over the chicken. Roll out the remaining pastry on a lightly floured surface, and cut out the lid to 5 mm/^{1}/$_4$ inch wider than the dish.

5. Beat the remaining egg and brush the rim of the pastry case. Lay the pastry lid on top, pressing to seal. Knock the edges with the back of a knife to seal further. Cut a slit in the lid and brush with the egg.

6. Sprinkle with the poppy seeds and bake in the preheated oven for about 30 minutes, or until the pastry is golden brown. Serve with the onion and mixed salad leaves.

Ingredients

300 g/10^1/$_2$ oz ready-made shortcrust pastry
1 tbsp olive oil
1 leek, trimmed and sliced
175 g/6 oz piece bacon, cut into small dice
225 g/8 oz cooked boneless chicken meat
2 avocados, peeled, pitted and chopped
1 tbsp lemon juice
salt and freshly ground black pepper
2 large eggs
150 ml/^{1}/$_4$ pint natural yogurt
4 tbsp chicken stock
1 tbsp poppy seeds

To serve:
sliced red onion
mixed salad leaves

A Swedish-Finnish Visitor to England

'The art of cooking as practised by Englishmen does not extend much beyond roast beef and plum pudding.'

Pehr Kalm (1716–79)

Traditional Fish Pie

SERVES 4

1. Preheat the oven to 200°C/400°F/Gas Mark 6, about 15 minutes before cooking. Place the fish in a shallow frying pan, pour over 300 ml/½ pint of the milk and add the onion. Season to taste with salt and pepper. Bring to the boil and simmer for 8–10 minutes until the fish is cooked. Remove the fish with a slotted spoon and place in a 1.4 litre/2½ pint baking dish. Strain the cooking liquid and reserve.

2. Boil the potatoes until soft, then mash with 40 g/1½ oz of the butter and 2–3 tablespoons of the remaining milk. Reserve.

3. Arrange the prawns and quartered eggs on top of the fish, then scatter over the sweetcorn and sprinkle with the parsley.

4. Melt the remaining butter in a saucepan, stir in the flour and cook gently for 1 minute, stirring. Whisk in the reserved cooking liquid and remaining milk. Cook for 2 minutes, or until thickened, then pour over the fish mixture and cool slightly.

5. Spread the mashed potato over the top of the pie and sprinkle over the grated cheese. Bake in the oven for 30 minutes until golden. Serve immediately.

Ingredients

450 g/1 lb cod or coley fillets, skinned
450 ml/¾ pint milk
1 small onion, peeled and quartered
salt and freshly ground black pepper
900 g/2 lb potatoes, peeled and cut into chunks
100 g/3½ oz butter
125 g/4 oz large prawns
2 large eggs, hard-boiled and quartered
198 g can sweetcorn, drained
2 tbsp freshly chopped parsley
3 tbsp plain flour
50 g/2 oz Cheddar cheese, grated

Fishy Facts

It is useful to know that:

1. A lobster is really fresh if it has a stiff tail.

2. You can draw off some of the saltiness from anchovies by soaking them in milk for an hour.

3. If you bake fillets of fish on lettuce leaves they do not stick to your tray, and the fillets stay moist as well.

4. If you thread prawns onto skewers lengthways they will not curl up during cooking.

5. The correct way to eat caviar is on cold toast; hot toast makes the caviar melt and go all runny!

Sausage & Mash

SERVES 4

1. Melt the butter with the oil and add the onions. Cover and cook gently for about 20 minutes until the onions have collapsed. Add the sugar and stir well. Uncover and continue to cook, stirring often, until the onions are very soft and golden. Add the thyme, stir well, then add the flour, stirring. Gradually add the Madeira and the stock. Bring to the boil and simmer gently for 10 minutes.

2. Meanwhile, put the sausages in a large frying pan and cook over a medium heat for 15–20 minutes, turning often, until golden brown and slightly sticky all over.

3. For the mashed potatoes, boil the potatoes in plenty of lightly salted water for 15–18 minutes until tender. Drain well and return to the saucepan. Put the saucepan over a low heat to allow the potatoes to dry thoroughly. Remove from the heat and add the butter, crème fraîche and salt and pepper. Mash thoroughly. Serve the mashed potatoes topped with the sausages and onion gravy.

Ingredients

50 g/2 oz butter
1 tbsp olive oil
2 large onions, peeled and thinly sliced
pinch sugar
1 tbsp freshly chopped thyme
1 tbsp plain flour
100 ml/3½ fl oz Madeira
200 ml/7 fl oz vegetable stock
8–12 good-quality butchers' pork sausages,
   depending on size

For the mashed potatoes:
6–8 floury potatoes, peeled
75 g/3 oz butter
4 tbsp crème fraîche
salt and freshly ground black pepper

Bread & Butter Pudding

SERVES 4-6

1. Preheat the oven to 180°C/350°F/Gas Mark 4, 10 minutes before cooking. Lightly butter a 1.1 litre/2 pint ovenproof dish. Butter the bread and cut into quarters. Arrange half the bread in the dish and scatter over two thirds of the dried fruit and sugar. Repeat the layering, finishing with the dried fruit.

2. Beat the eggs and milk together and pour over the bread and butter. Leave to stand for 30 minutes.

3. Sprinkle with the remaining sugar and a little nutmeg and carefully place in the oven. Cook for 40 minutes, or until the pudding has lightly set and the top is golden.

4. Remove and sprinkle with a little extra sugar, if liked. Serve with freshly made custard.

Ingredients

2–3 tbsp unsalted butter, softened
4–6 slices white bread
75 g/3 oz mixed dried fruit
25 g/1 oz caster sugar, plus extra
   for sprinkling
2 medium eggs
450 ml/³/₄ pint semi-skimmed
   milk, warmed
freshly grated nutmeg
freshly made custard, to serve

Crunchy Rhubarb Crumble

1. Preheat the oven to 180°C/350°F/Gas Mark 4. Place the flour in a large bowl and cut the butter into cubes. Add to the flour and rub in with the fingertips until the mixture looks like fine breadcrumbs, or blend for a few seconds in a food processor.

2. Stir in the rolled oats, demerara sugar, sesame seeds and cinnamon. Mix well and reserve.

3. Prepare the rhubarb by removing the thick ends of the stalks and cut diagonally into 2.5 cm/1 inch chunks. Wash thoroughly and pat dry with a clean tea towel. Place the rhubarb in a 1.1 litre/2 pint pie dish.

4. Sprinkle the caster sugar over the rhubarb and top with the reserved crumble mixture. Level the top of the crumble so that all the fruit is well covered and press down firmly. If liked, sprinkle the top with a little extra caster sugar.

5. Place on a baking sheet and bake in the preheated oven for 40–50 minutes until the fruit is soft and the topping is golden brown. Sprinkle the pudding with some more caster sugar and serve hot with custard or cream.

Ingredients

50 g/2 oz butter, softened
50 g/2 oz rolled oats
50 g/2 oz demerara sugar
1 tbsp sesame seeds
½ tsp ground cinnamon
450 g/1 lb fresh rhubarb
50 g/2 oz caster sugar, plus extra
    for more sprinkling
custard or cream, to serve

Table Etiquette

'Man, it has been said, is a dining animal.
Creatures of the inferior races eat and drink; man only dines.'

from *Mrs Beeton's Book of Household Management*, 1861, by Isabella Beeton (1836–65)

Here are some tips to remember when wishing to behave properly at the dinner table:

1. With cutlery you should always work your way from the outside inwards.

2. Men should stand when women leave the table and then again when they return.

3. Finish your mouthful before taking a sip of drink.

4. Try not to have your elbows resting on the table whilst you are eating.

5. Don't push food onto your spoon or fork with your fingers.

6. Food should be passed to the right.

7. A woman should excuse herself if she wishes to reapply her lipstick after a meal.

8. If you get up, place your napkin on your chair, not the table.

9. Soup should be spooned away from you, with the bowl tilted away from body.

10. If you spill something on someone, offer them a napkin to clean themselves up rather than dabbing at it yourself.

Classic Flapjacks

MAKES 12

1. Preheat the oven to 160°C/325°F/Gas Mark 3. Butter a 20.5 cm/8 inch square baking tin.

2. Place the butter, sugar and golden syrup in a saucepan and heat gently until the butter has melted and every grain of sugar has dissolved.

3. Remove from the heat and stir in the oats and vanilla extract. Stir well and then spoon the mixture into the prepared tin.

4. Smooth level with the back of a large spoon. Bake in the centre of the preheated oven for 30–40 minutes until golden. Leave to cool in the tin for 10 minutes, then mark into fingers and leave in the tin until completely cold. When cold, cut into fingers with a sharp knife.

Ingredients

175 g/6 oz butter, plus extra for greasing
125 g/4 oz demerara sugar
2 tbsp golden syrup
175 g/6 oz jumbo porridge oats
few drops vanilla extract

Scottish Shortbread

SERVES 4

1. Preheat the oven to 120°C/250°F/Gas Mark ½, 10 minutes before baking. Lightly grease two 20–23 cm/8–9 inch cake or tart tins with removable bases. Sift the plain flour, rice flour and salt into a bowl and reserve.

2. Using an electric mixer, beat the butter for about 1 minute in a large bowl until creamy. Add the sugars and continue beating for 1–2 minutes until very light and fluffy. If using, beat in the vanilla extract.

3. Using a wooden spoon, stir the flour mixture into the butter and sugar until well blended. Turn onto a lightly floured surface and knead lightly to blend completely.

4. Divide the dough evenly between the two tins, smoothing the surface. Using a fork, press 2 cm/¾ inch radiating lines around the edge of the dough. Lightly sprinkle the surfaces with a little sugar, then prick the surface lightly with the fork.

5. Using a sharp knife, mark each dough round into eight wedges. Bake in the preheated oven for 50–60 minutes until pale golden and crisp. Cool in the tins on a wire rack for about 5 minutes.

6. Carefully remove the side of each pan and slide the bottoms onto a heatproof surface. Using the knife marks as a guide, cut each shortbread into eight wedges while still warm. Cool completely on the wire rack, then store in airtight containers.

Ingredients

225 g/8 oz plain flour
60 g/2 oz rice flour
¼ tsp salt
175 g/6 oz unsalted butter, softened
60 g/2 oz caster sugar
25 g/1 oz icing sugar, sifted
¼ tsp vanilla extract (optional)
sugar, for sprinkling

Jam Roly Poly

SERVES 6

1. Preheat the oven to 200°C/400°F/Gas Mark 6. Make the pastry by sifting the flour and salt into a large bowl. Add the suet and mix lightly, then add about 150 ml/1/4 pint water a little at a time and mix to form a soft and pliable dough. (Take care not to make the dough too wet.)

2. Turn the dough out on to a lightly floured board and knead gently until smooth. Roll the dough out into a 23 cm/9 inch x 28 cm/11 inch rectangle.

3. Spread the jam over the dough, leaving a border of 1 cm/1/2 inch all round. Fold the border over the jam and brush the edges with water. Lightly roll the rectangle up from one of the short sides, seal the top edge and press the ends together. (Do not roll the pudding up too tightly.)

4. Turn the pudding upside down on to a large piece of greaseproof paper large enough to come halfway up the sides. (If using nonstick baking parchment, then oil lightly.) Tie the ends of the paper, to make a boat-shaped paper case for the pudding to sit in and to leave plenty of room for it to expand.

5. Brush the pudding lightly with milk and sprinkle with the sugar. Bake in the preheated oven for 30–40 minutes until well risen and golden. Serve immediately with the jam sauce.

Ingredients

225 g/8 oz self-raising flour
1/4 tsp salt
125 g/4 oz shredded suet
3 tbsp strawberry jam
1 tbsp milk, to glaze
1 tsp caster sugar
ready-made jam sauce, to serve

Spotted Dick

1. Mix together the flour, breadcrumbs, suet, lemon zest, and caster sugar in a large bowl and then add the currants. Slowly add the lemon juice with sufficient milk to make a soft, but not sticky, dough.

2. Flour a board well and place the dough on top. Shape it into a roll about 18 cm/ 7 inches in length. Wrap in a well-floured pudding cloth or double piece of muslin, or in greaseproof paper and then kitchen foil.

3. Place in the top of a steamer standing over a saucepan of gently boiling water. Steam steadily for 1½–2 hours until the roll feels firm when pushed with your finger.

4. When the pudding is finished, remove from the steamer and unwrap carefully. Place it on a warm serving dish and serve with freshly made custard.

Ingredients

125 g/4 oz self-raising flour, plus
    extra for dusting
125 g/4 oz fresh white breadcrumbs
125 g/4 oz vegetable suet
juice and grated zest of 1 large
    lemon, preferably unwaxed
50 g/2 oz caster sugar
175 g/6 oz currants
85–125 ml/3–4 fl oz semi-
    skimmed milk
freshly made custard, to serve

Summer Pavlova

1. Preheat the oven to 150°C/300°F/Gas Mark 2. Line a baking sheet with a sheet of greaseproof paper or baking parchment.

2. Place the egg whites in a clean, grease-free bowl and whisk until very stiff. Whisk in half the sugar, the vanilla extract, vinegar and cornflour, and continue whisking until stiff. Gradually, whisk in the remaining sugar, a teaspoonful at a time until very stiff and glossy.

3. Using a large spoon, arrange spoonfuls of the meringue in a circle on the greaseproof paper or baking parchment. Bake in the oven for 1 hour until crisp and dry. Turn the oven off and leave the meringue in the oven to cool completely.

4. Remove the meringue from the baking sheet and peel away the paper. Mix together the yogurt and honey. Place the pavlova on a serving plate and spoon the yogurt into the centre. Scatter over the strawberries, raspberries, blueberries and kiwis. Dust with the icing sugar and serve.

Ingredients

4 medium egg whites
225 g/8 oz caster sugar
1 tsp vanilla extract
2 tsp white wine vinegar
1½ tsp cornflour
300 ml/½ pint half-fat Greek-set yogurt
2 tbsp honey
225 g/8 oz strawberries, hulled
125 g/4 oz raspberries
125 g/4 oz blueberries
4 kiwis, peeled and sliced
icing sugar, to decorate

Classic Pimm's

SERVES 8-10

This is one of the most well known and much loved punches of all. Pimm's is gin-based and although its recipe is a closely guarded secret, it is possible to detect subtle aromas of spices and citrus fruits. There are five other Pimm's available and the main difference is the base alcohol used.

1. Pour the Pimm's and lemonade into a large glass serving jug and add the ice cubes, the cucumber and prepared fruits.

2. Stir well before adding the borage or mint sprigs. Leave for the flavours to infuse, at least 10 minutes then serve in tall glasses with spoons

Alternative

When wishing to serve a single glass of Pimm's, use one measure of Pimm's to one measure of lemonade or soda water. Use as much or as little fruit as preferred.

Ingredients

300 ml/^{1}/$_2$ pint Pimm's No 1
700 ml/23^1/$_2$ fl oz lemonade
small piece cucumber, thinly sliced
^{1}/$_2$ orange, thinly sliced and each slice cut in half
^{1}/$_2$ red or green apple, cored and sliced
6 strawberries, lightly rinsed and sliced if large
2-3 sprigs borage or mint
10-12 ice cubes

Iced Bakewell Tart

SERVES 8

1. Preheat the oven to 200°C/400°F/Gas Mark 6. Place the flour and salt in a bowl, rub in the butter and vegetable fat until the mixture resembles breadcrumbs. Alternatively, blend quickly, in short bursts in a food processor.

2. Add the eggs with sufficient water to make a soft, pliable dough. Knead lightly on a floured board then chill in the refrigerator for about 30 minutes. Roll out the pastry and use to line a 23 cm/9 inch loose-bottomed flan tin.

3. For the filling, mix together the melted butter, sugar, almonds and beaten eggs and add a few drops of almond extract. Spread the base of the pastry case with the raspberry jam and spoon over the egg mixture.

4. Bake in the preheated oven for about 30 minutes, or until the filling is firm and golden brown. Remove from the oven and allow to cool completely.

5. When the tart is cold, make the icing by mixing together the icing sugar and lemon juice, a little at a time, until the icing is smooth and of a spreadable consistency. Spread the icing over the tart, leave to set for 2–3 minutes and sprinkle with the almonds. Chill in the refrigerator for about 10 minutes and serve.

Ingredients

For the rich pastry:
175 g/6 oz plain flour
pinch salt
60 g/2½ oz butter, cut into small pieces
50 g/2 oz white vegetable fat, cut into small pieces
2 small egg yolks, beaten

For the filling:
125 g/4 oz butter, melted
125 g/4 oz caster sugar
125 g/4 oz ground almonds
2 large eggs, beaten
few drops almond extract
2 tbsp seedless raspberry jam

For the icing:
125 g/4 oz icing sugar, sifted
6–8 tsp fresh lemon juice
25 g/1 oz toasted flaked almonds

A Grace Before Dinner

O Thou who kindly dost provide
For every creature's want!
We bless Thee, God of Nature wide,
For all Thy goodness lent:
And if it please Thee, heavenly Guide,
May never worse be sent;
But, whether granted or denied,
Lord, bless us with content. Amen!

by Robert Burns (1759–96)

Lemon Meringue Pie

SERVES 4-6

1. Preheat the oven to 200°C/400°F/Gas Mark 6 and place a baking sheet in the oven to heat. Sift the flour and salt into a bowl or a food processor, and add the lard and butter, cut into small pieces. Rub in with your fingertips, or process, until the mixture resembles fine crumbs. Mix in 2–3 tablespoons cold water to form a soft dough, then knead lightly until smooth. Grease a 20.5 cmm/8 inch round flan tin. Roll out the pastry on a lightly floured surface and use to line the tin. Chill for 30 minutes while you make the filling.

2. Put the zest and granulated sugar with 300 ml/$\frac{1}{2}$ pint water in a heavy-based pan over a low heat and stir until the sugar has completely dissolved. Blend the cornflour with the lemon juice to a smooth paste, then add to the pan and bring to a boil, stirring all the time. Boil for 2 minutes, then remove from the heat and beat in the egg yolks. Set aside to cool.

3. Prick the pastry case, line with greaseproof paper and pour in baking beans. Place on the baking sheet and bake for 10 minutes. Remove from the oven and lift out the paper and beans. Bake the pastry for a further 10 minutes. Remove from the oven, spoon the lemon filling into the pastry case and set aside. Reduce the oven temperature to 150°C/300°F/Gas Mark 2.

Ingredients

175 g/6 oz plain flour
pinch salt
40 g/1$\frac{1}{2}$ oz lard or white vegetable fat
40 g/1$\frac{1}{2}$ oz butter or block margarine

For the filling:
grated zest and juice of 2 lemons
75 g/3 oz granulated sugar
40 g/1$\frac{1}{2}$ oz cornflour
2 large egg yolks

For the topping:
2 large egg whites
125 g/4 oz caster sugar

4. Whisk the egg whites in a clean, dry bowl until very stiff. Whisk in half the caster sugar a little at a time, then fold in the remainder. Spread over the lemon filling, making sure it covers the top, right to the edges of the filling. Bake for 30 minutes until the meringue is golden. Leave to 'settle' for 20 minutes before serving, or eat cold on the day of baking.

Top Tip

Always remember to double check that the bowl being used to whisk egg whites is completely clean, as you will find that any grease will prevent the egg whites from rising into the stiff consistency necessary for this recipe.

Baked Apple Dumplings

SERVES 4

1. Preheat the oven to 200°C/400°F/Gas Mark 6. Lightly oil a baking tray. Place the flour and salt in a bowl and stir in the suet.

2. Add just enough water to the mixture to mix to a soft but not sticky dough, using the fingertips.

3. Turn the dough on to a lightly floured board and knead lightly into a ball. Divide the dough into four pieces and roll out each piece into a thin square, large enough to encase the apples.

4. Peel and core the apples and place 1 apple in the centre of each square of pastry. Fill the centre of the apple with mincemeat, brush the edges of each pastry square with water and draw the corners up to meet over each apple.

5. Press the edges of the pastry firmly together and decorate with pastry leaves and shapes made from the extra pastry trimmings.

6. Place the apples on the prepared baking tray, brush with the egg white and sprinkle with the sugar.

7. Bake in the preheated oven for 30 minutes or until golden and the pastry and apples are cooked. Serve the dumplings hot with the custard or vanilla sauce.

Ingredients

225 g/8 oz self-raising flour
$\frac{1}{4}$ tsp salt
125 g/4 oz shredded suet
4 medium cooking apples
4–6 tsp luxury mincemeat
1 medium egg white, beaten
2 tsp caster sugar
custard or vanilla sauce,
   to serve

Recipe for Homemade Custard

To make homemade custard, pour 600 ml/1 pint milk with a few drops of
vanilla extract into a saucepan and bring to the boil.

Remove from the heat and allow to cool.

Meanwhile, whisk 5 egg yolks and 3 tablespoons caster sugar together
in a mixing bowl until thick and pale in colour.

Add the milk, stir and strain into a heavy-based saucepan. Cook the custard
on a low heat, stirring constantly until the consistency of double cream.

Pour over your desired dessert.

Fresh Strawberry Victoria Sponge

SERVES 8-10

1. Preheat the oven to 190°C/375°F/Gas Mark 5, 10 minutes before baking. Lightly oil and line the bases of two 20.5 cm/8 inch round cake tins with greaseproof paper or baking parchment.

2. Using an electric whisk, beat the butter, sugar and vanilla extract until pale and fluffy. Gradually beat in the eggs a little at a time, beating well between each addition. Sift half the flour over the mixture and using a metal spoon or rubber spatula gently fold into the mixture. Sift over the remaining flour and fold in until just blended.

3. Divide the mixture between the tins, spreading evenly. Gently smooth the surfaces with the back of a spoon. Bake in the centre of the preheated oven for 20–25 minutes until well risen and golden. Remove, leave to cool, then turn out on to a wire rack. Whip the cream with 1 tablespoon of the icing sugar until it forms soft peaks. Fold in the chopped strawberries.

4. Spread one cake layer evenly with the mixture and top with the second cake layer, rounded side up. Thickly dust the cake with icing sugar and decorate with the reserved strawberries. Carefully slide on to a serving plate and serve.

Ingredients

175 g/6 oz unsalted butter, softened
175 g/6 oz caster sugar
1 tsp vanilla extract
3 large eggs, beaten
175 g/6 oz self-raising flour
150 ml/¹/₄ pint double cream
2 tbsp icing sugar, sifted
225 g/8 oz fresh strawberries, hulled and chopped
few extra strawberries, to decorate

Dundee Cake

SERVES 8-10

1. Preheat the oven to 180°C/350°F/Gas Mark 4. Grease and line the bottom of an 18 cm/7 inch deep round cake tin with nonstick baking parchment.

2. Place the dried fruit in a bowl and stir in the ground almonds to coat the fruit.

3. Grate the zest finely from the lemon into the bowl, then squeeze out 1 tablespoon of juice and add to the same bowl. In another bowl, beat the butter and sugar together until light and fluffy. Beat in the eggs a little at a time, adding 1 teaspoon flour with each addition.

4. Sift in the remaining flour, then add the fruit and almond mixture. Fold together with a large metal spoon until smooth. Spoon the mixture into the tin and make a dip in the centre with the back of a spoon. Arrange the almonds over the top in circles.

5. Bake for 1 hour, then reduce the heat to 150°C/300°F/Gas Mark 2 and bake for a further hour or until a skewer inserted into the centre comes out clean. Cool in the tin for 5 minutes, then turn out to cool on a wire rack.

Ingredients

400 g/14 oz mixed dried fruit
50 g/2 oz ground almonds
1 lemon
150 g/5 oz butter, softened
150 g/5 oz natural golden
 caster sugar
3 medium eggs, beaten
125 g/4 oz plain flour
40 g/1½ oz whole blanched
 almonds

Orange Curd & Plum Puddings

SERVES 4

1. Preheat the oven to 200°C/400°F/Gas Mark 6. Lightly oil a 20.5 cm/8 inch round cake tin. Cook the plums with 2 tablespoons of the light brown sugar for 8–10 minutes to soften them, remove from the heat and reserve.

2. Mix together the lemon zest, butter and oil. Lay a sheet of pastry in the prepared cake tin and brush with the lemon zest mixture.

3. Cut the sheets of filo pastry in half and then place one half sheet in the cake tin and brush again.

4. Top with the remaining halved sheets of pastry brushing each time with the lemon zest mixture. Fold each sheet in half lengthwise to line the sides of the tin to make a filo case.

5. Mix together the plums, orange curd and sultanas and spoon into the pastry case.

6. Draw the pastry edges up over the filling to enclose. Brush the remaining sheets of filo pastry with the lemon zest mixture and cut into thick strips.

7. Scrunch each strip of pastry and arrange on top of the pie. Bake in the preheated oven for 25 minutes, until golden. Sprinkle with icing sugar and serve with the Greek yogurt.

Ingredients

700 g/1½ lb plums, stoned and quartered
2 tbsp light brown sugar
grated zest of ½ lemon
25 g/1 oz butter, melted
1 tbsp olive oil
6 sheets filo pastry
½ x 411 g jar luxury orange curd
50 g/2 oz sultanas
icing sugar, to decorate
thick set Greek yogurt, to serve

Luxury Mince Pies

MAKES 20

i. Sift the flour and ground almonds into a bowl or a food processor and add the butter. Rub in, or process, until the mixture resembles fine crumbs. Sift in the icing sugar and stir in the lemon zest. Whisk the egg yolk and milk together in a separate bowl and stir into the mixture until a soft dough forms. Wrap the pastry in clingfilm and chill for 30 minutes.

2. Preheat the oven to 200°C/400°F/Gas Mark 6. Grease two 12-hole patty tins. Roll out the pastry on a lightly floured surface to 3 mm/⅛ inch thickness. Cut out 20 rounds using a 7.5 cm/3 inch fluted round pastry cutter. Re-roll the trimmings into thin strips.

3. Mix the filling ingredients together in a bowl. Place 1 tablespoon of the filling in each pastry case, then dampen the edges of each case with a little water. Put four strips of pastry over the top of each case to form a lattice.

4. Bake for 10–15 minutes until the pastry is crisp. Dust with icing sugar and serve hot or cold.

Ingredients

275 g/10 oz plain flour
25 g/1 oz ground almonds
175 g/6 oz butter, diced
75 g/3 oz icing sugar
finely grated zest of 1 lemon
1 egg yolk
3 tbsp milk

For the filling:
225 g/8 oz mincemeat
1 tbsp dark rum or orange juice
finely grated zest of 1 orange
75 g/3 oz dried cranberries

icing sugar, for dusting

Publisher's Note:
Raw or semicooked eggs should not be consumed by babies, toddlers,
pregnant or breast-feeding women, the elderly or people with a chronic illness.

Publisher & Creative Director: Nick Wells
Editorial: Laura Bulbeck
Art Director: Mike Spender
Layout Design: Jane Ashley
Digital Design & Production: Chris Herbert

Special thanks to: Catherine Taylor, Digby Smith, Helen Wall and Laura Zats

First published in 2012 by
FLAME TREE PUBLISHING
Crabtree Hall, Crabtree Lane
Fulham, London SW6 6TY
United Kingdom
www.flametreepublishing.com

Flame Tree is part of The Foundry Creative Media Company Limited

12 14 16 15 13
1 3 5 7 9 10 8 6 4 2

ISBN: 978-0-85775-382-3

A copy of the CIP data for this book is available from the British Library.

Picture Credits
All images courtesy of Foundry Arts except for the following, which are © Fine Art Photographic Library:
5 Joseph Moseley Barber (fl. 1858–89), *A Farmhouse Kitchen*; 15 artist unknown, *Fashion Plate – Queen Victoria & The Duke
Of Wellington In Windsor*; 16 artist unknown, *A Joyous New Year*; 20 George Goodwin Kilburne (1839–1924), *Tea-Time*;
25 George Armfield (1806–93), *The Keeper's Cottage*; 27 Jacques-Laurent Agasse (1767–1849), *The Fish Shop*; 31 Samuel
Sidley (1829–96), *Saying Grace*, 1872; 39 Edmund Swift, *Saying Grace*; 43 William MacDuff (1824–81), *Christmas At
Home, Stirring the Christmas Pudding*, 1860
and courtesy of Shutterstock:
8 © Maria Dryfhout; recurring decorations © asel; bioraven; Canicula

Front cover artwork based on images courtesy of Shutterstock and © Aleksey Vl B.; JaneH

Printed in China